W9-DEJ-063

291.13
JAP
Japanese gods and myths

ON LINE

MORRIS AUTOMATED INFORMATION NETWORK

0 1014 0080140 9

JUN   2000

JEFFERSON TWP PUBLIC LIBRARY
1031 WELDON RD
OAK RIDGE, NJ 07438-9511
(973) 208-6115 6244

DEMCO

Japanese Gods
and Myths

JAPANESE GODS AND MYTHS

Jefferson Twp. Public Library
1031 Weldon Road
Oak Ridge, NJ 07438
(973) 208-6115

**CHARTWELL
BOOKS, INC.**

Published by Chartwell Books
A Division of Book Sales Inc.
114 Northfield Avenue
Edison, New Jersey 08837
USA

Copyright ©1998 Quantum Books Ltd
This edition printed in 1999

All rights reserved.
This book is protected by copyright. No part of it may be
reproduced, stored in a retrieval system, or transmitted in
any form or by any means, without the prior permission in
writing of the Publisher, nor be otherwise circulated in any
form of binding or cover other than that in which it is
published and without a similar condition including this
condition being imposed on the subsequent publisher.

ISBN 0-7858-1080-3

This book is produced by
Quantum Books Ltd
6 Blundell Street
London N7 9BH

Project Manager: Rebecca Kingsley
Project Editor: Judith Millidge
Designer: Wayne Humphries

The material in this publication previously appeared in
*The Atlas of Languages, The Book of the Sun, Chinese
Brush Painting, Journey Through Japan, Oriental
Mythology*

QUMJG&M
Set in Times
Reproduced in Singapore by Eray Scan
Printed in Singapore by Star Standard Industries (Pte) Ltd

CONTENTS

THE ROOTS
OF RELIGION

Traditional Shinto, as opposed to state Shintoism, has its origin about 2000 years ago. Shinto is Japan's primal religion and is integrated into Japan's culture. In the 3rd century B.C., a Japan consisting of a single race and a single language emerged after a long period of racial and cultural diversity. The political unification of Japan was completed in the 6th century A.D., when the Yamato clan (the Emperor Akihito is a direct descendant) achieved superiority over its peers, consigning the gods and ancestors of other tribes to the darkest recesses of Japanese mythology.

Each clan had its own ancestors who had achieved divine status, and with Yamato overlordship from the 6th century, Yamato ancestors received national recognition,

In 1989, the enthronement ceremony of Emperor Akihito was carried out according to Shinto tradition, as the emperor has always been the head of Japan's national religion. But opposition parties in Japan's democracy strongly criticized the idea of employing Shinto religions in the ceremonies concerning Emperor Hirohito's funeral and the coronation of his successor. State Shintoism is a relatively new phenomenon, which was started about 150 years ago in order to unify Japan after a long period of fractured feudalism. It took only a few decades for this artificial state Shintoism to get out of control, and the emperor's position as a human-god was abused (mostly by the army) to justify the state

Left: The head of Haniwa, a grave figurine dating from the 6th century A.D.

Right: The Izumo shrine, the oldest Shinto shrine in Japan. The Shinto gods are believed to assemble here every year in October, and so October is known as the "godless month" everywhere else.

invasion of neighboring countries. It is from Shinto that the authentic Japanese mythology comes, particularly from the *Kojiki*, the "Record of Ancient Things" (completed in the 8th century A.D.), which became a kind of statement of Shinto orthodoxy.

BIRTH OF A NATION

Japan's birth as a nation coincided with the start of rice-growing – Japan's main industry until quite recently – and Shinto consisted of rituals to pray for a good harvest, keeping the community unified through those ceremonies. The fact that people were primarily considered as members of the community rather than as individuals explains Shinto's survival despite the powerful influence of Buddhism: more than 70 percent of the Japanese still

worked in agriculture up to the end of the Second World War.

NATIVE JAPANESE

The original inhabitants of Japan were animists - that is, they worshiped aspects of nature. In the 4th century A.D., shamanistic immigrants crossed the Korean Straits and brought with them beliefs that the world was inhabited by good and evil spirits who could be controlled or propitiated by a tribal shaman or medicine man. The invaders forced the aboriginal Ainu tribe into the north of Japan, and defeated the southern peoples, gradually assimilating the original tribes and their native beliefs into their own culture. By the 6th century, Japan's population consisted of a disunited group of tribes who followed the

Above: Rice has been one of Japan's staple crops for centuries. Rice seedlings are planted during the rainy season.

Right: The modern work ethic in Japan strives to foster a strong community spirit, just as the Shinto religion does.

Far right: A beautiful example of calligraphy from the late Heian period. The flourishing of calligraphy in Japan was strongly influenced by Zen Buddhism.

世界から指名される製品を生みだそう。
CREATE QUALITY PRODUCTS DEMANDED BY THE WORLD.

Opposite page: A modern Samurai festival, commemorating the ancient "way of the warrior." Samurai warriors lived according to a strict code of ethics.

Far left: The statue of Buddha in the Todaji Temple, Nara. Emperor Shomu had this temple constructed in 745, and it took seven years to complete. Still standing, it is one of the biggest wooden buildings in the world, and fittingly, the statue of Buddha, which stands at over 25 meters tall, is the world's largest bronze statue.

Left: Kendo, "the way of the sword," is the art of fencing with bamboo swords, and developed from practice exercises in which Samurai warriors trained with bamboo sticks.

same broad religious practices, which became known as Shinto, or "the way of the gods."

SHINTO ETHICS

Agricultural life is hard physical work, and requires activity to be coordinated with the changing seasons. This integration of people's beliefs with their working lives still exists in Japanese companies today – it is a common practice to build small Shinto shrines on top of commercial buildings – but modern industrial work lacks the sensitivity to nature required for rice-growing. Nature and the changing seasons were not seen as romantic or beautiful, but life was lived according to the dictates of the seasons. So not surprisingly, the concepts of virtue in Shintoism are reflected in the success, or failure, of farming. The notions of purity, or clarity, and uncleanliness, or filth, are the most fundamental concepts in Shintoism; the word *kegare* is Japanese for

uncleanliness, and stems from *ke* meaning a mythical power to make things grow, and *gare* meaning lacking. Together, *kegare* therefore means a lack of power to make things (and particularly rice), and uncleanliness is thus associated with failure to thrive.

WRITTEN RECORDS

Writing probably did not arrive in Japan until it was introduced by Buddhist missionaries, sent by the king of Korea in 552 A.D. The Japanese immediately adopted the ancient Chinese system of writing and recording their religious beliefs. The main record of Shinto myth and historical legend is the *Kojiki,* the "Record of Ancient Things." completed in 712 A.D. It clearly shows influences from both Chinese and Indian Buddhism, but it is hard to tell exactly how strong these influences were as there is no written record of earlier, more ancient Shinto beliefs and practices. Divided

into three books, the first covering life with the gods; the second, dealings between humans and the gods; and the third, human life without the gods. It also traces the origins of the imperial clan and the leading families of Japan. The *Kojiki* was until recently regarded as sacred. Many of its stories involve these key concepts of purity and uncleanliness.

The most popular hero in the *Kojiki* is Yamato-takeru. His story is found in Book Two, which deals with man as he is about to depart from the world of the gods, and has the melancholic tone that characterizes so many Japanese epics.

BUDDHIST INFLUENCE

Buddhism was introduced to Japan from Korea in the middle of the 6th century. The first, and one of the most profound texts on Buddhism, *Giso,* appeared as early as the 7th century and was written by Shotoku Taishi, a member of

Above: The Golden Pavilion of Kinkakuji temple. This is an exact replica, built in 1955, of the 14th-century original which was destroyed by fire.

the imperial family who gave much support to the new religion. As is clear from the stories of the *Kojiki*, Shinto is a cult in which the spirit of every thing is worshiped, without a systematic structure or doctrine. Life after death is accepted, but early Shinto belief contained no moral teaching, or even the concept of reward or punishment after death. The term Shinto only came into use after the introduc-

tion of Buddhism to Japan, when it became necessary to differentiate between the two systems of belief.

"SHINTO WITH TWO FACES"
Although there was opposition to the spread of Buddhism, by the middle of the 8th century the two religions were closely intertwined. Kobo Taishi (774-834) introduced the doctrine

of Ryobu, or "Shinto with two faces," which permitted a compromise to be reached. For the next 1000 years Buddhist temples would contain Shinto shrines, and Shinto deities would be regarded as Buddhist guardians. Buddhist monks conducted the services at Shinto shrines (except at Izumo and Ise, where Amaterasu's shrine still exists). This happy coexistence came to an end at the beginning of the Meiji Restoration in 1868.

The Kamakura period (12th-14th centuries) was the heyday of Japanese chivalry, when the shoguns employed the samurai as their bodyguards. The samurai, who were not aristocrats but mostly came from farming backgrounds, were well acquainted with the harsh realities of life.

ZEN BUDDHISM

They found in Zen Buddhism – which was introduced to Japan at the same time as *Jodo* – another route to the heart of Buddhism. The directness of Zen, "the spiritual cult of steel," held great appeal for the samurai warriors, who had neither the time nor inclination to under-take long study or indulge in abstract argument in order to achieve enlightenment.

ZEN DIALOGS

The purpose of Zen is to move beyond the realm of the intellect. Zen rejects the use of words to explain experience as mere substi-tute for reality. Zen is taught through a series of short, elliptical dialogs (*mondo*), which have been described as a duel between master and pupil, another reason perhaps for their appeal to the warriors.

ZEN PHILOSOPHY

When Joshu was asked about the fundamen-tal principle of Buddhism, he replied, "The cypress-tree in the courtyard in front of you." "You are talking of an objective symbol," said the pupil. "No, I am not talking of an objec-tive symbol." "Then," asked the monk again, "What is the ultimate principle of Buddhism?" "The cypress-tree in the courtyard in front of you," again replied Joshu.

Zen stresses above all the oneness of hu-manity and nature, and herein lies the reason

Below: "Landscape for Four Seasons," part of a long scroll painting in black ink by the artist Sesshu, painted in 1486.

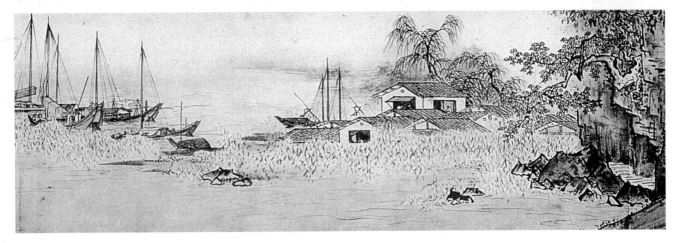

Above: A section from "Landscape for our Seasons." Like Chinese art, Japanese painting is noted for its meditative qualities.

Right: The Japanese tea ceremony, an ancient and formal tradition of hospitality. Drinking tea is regarded as "an adoration of the beautiful among the sordid facts of everyday existence."

why it has become the dominant school of Buddhism in Japan. The myths of the *Kojiki* demonstrate that familiarity with, and reverence toward, the natural world that are so strong in Japanese tradition. Not only is there no antagonism between Zen and the native Shinto sensibilities, but the different beliefs actually enhance one another. After being accepted by the numerically dominant samurai class, Zen started to permeate every single aspect of Japanese life.

It is impossible to talk about Japanese culture without mentioning Zen belief, which still permeates and heavily influences every area of creative activity: architecture (tea-houses), poetry (*haiku*), sports (archery and swordsmanship), painting (brush painting), gardening (stone gardens), theater (*Noh*), ceramics and food.

SHINTO ARCHITECTURE
Shinto architecture gave concrete form to the concept of purity, as exemplified in the stories of the *Kojiki*, and its simplicity and lack of abstraction also follow the precepts of Zen.

The Ise shrine, the central shrine of Shintoism, is situated in the deep forest beside a river whose water is crystal clear. The shrine occupies a vast area. The buildings are in the shape of a rice-storage house and all are made of bare wood, without paint or ornament, built on white pebble stones. Clear, straight lines dominate, with a few curves on the roofs. All the buildings, together with their various contents, are rebuilt every 20 years, thus ensuring that the necessary skills are transferred from generation to generation. This tradition goes back to ancient times. When they are newly built, the bare wood shines gold in the quiet, dark forest. The shrine shows us what an architect can express by employing only purely functional lines. The Ise shrine is the prototype of later Japanese architecture: the Katsura imperial villa, which was made in the 17th century, has much in common with the Ise shrine. This building, which was designed by Kobori Enshu, exemplifies the Japanese style of simplicity and functionality, and expresses an intense affinity with natural form and material.

Above: Hot alkaline springs near Kyushu, the first part of Japan to be subject to the marauding warriors of Kublai Khan in the 13th century.

RELIGION AND ART

As in religion, Japanese art was strongly influenced by Chinese Buddhism. In both China and Japan, artists became much admired as creative and inspired individuals, rather than regarded as mere artisans. Meditation is central to both Buddhist and Shinto thought, and landscape pictures painted on silk or parchment scrolls, became highly valued as aids to meditation in the early medieval period.

The high points for artistic activity in Japanese history – the Kamakura and Muromachi periods (1185-1568) – gave full expression to the spirit of Zen. But the manner and form that it took harked back to the period so lovingly recorded in the *Kojiki:* sculptures of angry Buddhist gods remind readers of the *Kojiki* hero Yamato-takeru, and the costumes of *Noh* plays display elegant designs that represent the plants that grow on the mountains and blossom in the fields where deities of the *Kojiki* once lived.

CREATION MYTHS

Previous page: A view of the extensive gardens of the Tofukugi temple, Kyoto.

Left: A large hanging scroll of a waterfall by Maruyama Okyo (1733-95). It was apparently commissioned by an abbot who needed a waterfall to meditate upon.

Book One of the *Kojiki* concerns itself with the creation. The cosmology of the *Kojiki* is a step-by-step evolution of the universe. There is no creation from absolute nothing by an absolute being. Although the following creation myth owes much to Chinese and Indian mythology, it is clearly the myth of an island race. The very simplicity and incoherence of the *Kojiki* is what its compilers intended, aiming to recreate the religious sense of ancient Japanese thought through a careful organization of prose and poetry. It is important to read the myths with imagination and faith, rather than looking for rational explanations to the stories.

THE BIRTH OF JAPAN

In the beginning, there was nothing but a shapeless egg of swirling gases. Slowly, the lighter areas rose up to form the heavens, and the darker, denser material sank to form the earth. Three gods created themselves, and hid in heaven. Landmasses floated about on the surface of the earth until eventually something appeared drifting between heaven and earth. It looked like the first shoot of a new reed and two gods were born from it, who also hid. Seven more gods were born in this way, the last two being Izanagi and Izanami.

IZANAGI AND IZANAMI

Izanagi and Izanami were commanded by the heavenly deities "to complete and solidify the drifting land" – in other words to form the Japanese islands. Standing on the "Floating Bridge of Heaven," they wondered whether there was anything below them, and so dipped the heavenly Jeweled Spear into the sea below to find out. They stirred the brine with a churning sound, and when they lifted up the spear again, the dripping brine from the tip of the spear piled up and became the island of Onokoro. Descending from the heavens, Izanagi and Izanami decided to make their home there, and stuck the spear into the ground to form the Heavenly Pillar.

THE CREATION OF THE LAND

Discovering that their bodies were differently formed, Izanagi asked his spouse Izanami if she was agreeable to giving birth to the land in order to produce more islands. When she agreed, they devised a marriage ritual: they walked around the Heavenly Pillar in opposite directions; when they met, Izanami said "How lovely! I have met a handsome man!" and then they made love.

Instead of producing an island, however, she gave birth to a deformed leech-child, which they cast adrift on the sea in a reed boat. They returned to heaven to consult the gods who told them that their mistake lay in the marriage ritual: Izanami should not have spoken first when they met around the pillar, as it is not a woman's place to initiate a conversation. In order to have children, they repeated the ritual, but this time, Izanagi spoke first.

On their return to earth, Izanagi and Izanami tried again and were successful. Over time, Izanami bore all the islands of Japan. They produced gods to beautify the islands, and also made gods of wind, trees, rivers, and mountains, completing the creation of Japan.

The last god produced by Izanami was the fire god, whose birth scorched her genitals so badly that she died. However, as she died, she continued to produce more gods from her vomit, urine, and excreta. Izanagi was so angry that he cut off the fire god's head, but drops of his blood fell on the earth, producing still more deities.

THE HEAVENLY PILLAR

There have been various interpretations of the ritual of circling around the Heavenly Pillar. Scholars of the late Edo period (from the 18th century to the early 19th century) regarded the pillar simply as a phallic symbol. It clearly resembles the European maypole, which is believed to capture the vital powers latent in a tree, and is also linked with the ancient Japanese belief that processions round tall trees are needed to summon down the deities who

Right: There are many varieties of pine tree in Japan, and they have peculiar significance in Japanese painting. Because the leaves do not fall or even change color, they have come to symbolize longevity, which is highly valued in Japan. This picture is ink on paper by Tohaku Hasegawa (1539-1616).

Overleaf: Waves at Matsushima *by Tawaraya Sotatsu (1575-1643), ink and gold on paper. This picture was produced during the Edo period, a highpoint of Japanese art.*

Above: The sacred dance hall of Kasuge shrine at Nara. Here the ritual Kagura dances are performed in honor of Amaterasu, the sun goddess.

live in the heavens or high mountains.

KOJIKI MYTHS

Until the scholar Motoori Norinaga discovered the importance of the *Kojiki* in the 18th century, it was regarded as far inferior to its contemporary, the *Nihon-shoki,* a history book completed in 720 A.D., eight years after the presentation of the *Kojiki.* The *Nihon-shoki* is in many ways more accessible than the *Kojiki*

as it presents its material in a more detached way. The *Kojiki,* on the other hand, invites the readers to have strong sympathy with the myths, and does not seem to care much about the coherence and logic of the stories it includes.

The *Kojiki* not only became the main source of authority for the Shinto religion, but in many senses it also reinforced the power of the emperor as well. The myths of the *Kojiki* reveal a three-layered cosmos. Firstly, the creation of Japan by Izanagi and Izanami, with the forces of life and fertility, followed by pollution and purification. Secondly, the supremacy of the glorious sun goddess Amaterasu, from whom the imperial line is descended. And thirdly, the rituals and chanting necessary to invoke the *kami,* or spirits.

When the *Kojiki* was written, the influence of China was starting to be apparent everywhere. The legal system, the arts, and literature were strongly affected. As the influence of Buddhism spread from China and Asia in the 6th century and became the dominant belief among the aristocracy, the *Kojiki* was important in recording Japanese life before foreign influences took too great a hold. The book portrayed an image of life filled with a strong sense of the unity of humanity with nature and god, and the unity between people through simple rituals. It also aimed to bring about clear national self-consciousness by using a lucid image of the past to overcome

Below: The Imperial Palace, Tokyo, the home of the emperors of Japan, and one of the few old buildings still standing in the city.

Right: A modern depiction of Amaterasu, goddess of the sun, emerging from the cave, lured out by the other gods.

the crisis of national identity, a crisis similar in some ways to the one Japan is facing today.

In the book, purity (or growth power) is exemplified by the story of the hero Yamato-takeru (see page 50). The opposite concept of *kegare* (or pollution) is illustrated by the story of Izanami's death:

THE HEARTH OF YOMI

After giving birth to numerous islands and other features of nature – waterfalls, mountains, trees, herbs, and the wind – Izanami died of a terrible fever. Izanagi followed her to Yomi, the land of the dead, but was too late: she had already eaten at the hearth of Yomi, which meant that her return to the land of the living was impossible. She asked Izanagi to wait for her patiently as she discussed with the gods whether she could return, but he could not. Impatiently, he threw down the comb he was wearing and set light to it, and then he entered the hall. What he saw was dreadful:

"Maggots were squirming and roaring in Izanami's corpse. In her head was Great-Thunder; in her breast was Fire-Thunder; in her belly was Black-Thunder; in her genitals was Crack-Thunder; in her right hand was Earth-Thunder; in her left foot was Sounding-Thunder; in her right foot was Reclining-Thunder. Altogether there were eight thunder deities."

THE AFTERLIFE

As can be seen from the above description of the land of the dead, ancient Japanese ideas about death and the afterlife contained no thought of a final judgement. The land of the dead, Yomi, is one of filth and uncleanliness

rather than of horror or punishment. By eating from the hearth of Yomi, Izanami was forbidden to return to the land of the living. The scholar Norinaga considered that this was because food cooked with the fire of Yomi became impure. A simpler interpretation is that Izanami, having eaten the food of Yomi, had become a person of Yomi. The idea that one cannot return home after having eaten the food of the afterlife – or even of a foreign land – is a common one throughout the world.

In the final passage of the relationship between Izanami and Izanagi, the concept of mortality for humankind is introduced. The use of peaches as a weapon is a sign of Chinese influence on the *Kojiki*. In China, peaches and peach trees have from antiquity been used to dispel demons and evil spirits. The peach is furthermore often used as a symbol of longevity (see below).

DEATH COMES TO THE WORLD

Izanagi was frightened by the sight of Izanami, and he turned and fled. Shamed by his actions, Izanami sent the hags of Yomi to pursue him, but he evaded them, using magic tricks. When Izanagi arrived at the border between the land of the living and the underworld, he attacked his pursuers with three peaches he had found nearby. They all retreated as fast as they could. Then Izanagi said to all the peaches: "Just as you have saved me, when any of the race of mortal men fall into painful straits and suffer in anguish, then you will save them also."

THE PURSUIT OF IZANAGI

Finally Izanami herself came in pursuit of Izanagi. He pulled a huge bolder across the pass from Yomi to the land of the living, and Izanagi and Izanami stood facing each other on either side of the bolder. Izanami then said: "O my beloved husband, if you do thus, I will each day strangle to death 1000 of the populace of your country." To this Izanagi replied: "O my beloved spouse, if you do this, I will each day build 1500 parturition huts," meaning that this number of people would be born. She told him that he must accept her death, and Izanagi promised not to visit her again. Then, they formally declared their marriage at an end.

THE CHILDREN OF IZANAMI AND IZANUGI

Thus the marriage of Izanami and Izanagi brought the natural world into existence, and their separation, or "divorce," is the beginning of mortality. On his return to the land of the living, Izanagi rid himself of the sullying effects of his descent into the underworld by undergoing purification.

THE CREATION OF THE GODS

"He arrived at the plain by the river-mouth, where he took off his clothes and the articles worn on his body. As each item was flung on to the ground, a deity came into existence. And as Izanagi entered the water to wash himself, yet more gods were created." Finally, the most important gods in the Japanese pantheon were created when he washed his face. When he wiped his left eye, Amaterasu, the sun goddess, was born; the moon god Tsuki-yomi emerged from his right eye, and the storm god Susano from his nose.

Izanagi decided to divide the world between his three children, instructing Amaterasu to rule heaven, Tsuki-yomi to rule the night, and Susano to rule the seas. Susano, however, said he would rather go to the underworld with his dead mother, so Izanagi banished him, then withdrew from the world to live in high heaven.

Above: The annual Jidai festival in Kyoto. Participants dress in costumes representing styles from the 8th to the 19th centuries, celebrating the city's time as Japan's capital.

RELIGIOUS SYMBOLISM

Izanagi's act of cleansing *(misogi)* shows how vital force can be recovered by purification. In the same way that rice-growing follows a cycle in which both the land and the people become exhausted, and are then revitalized by water or a period of rest, so Izanagi regains his strength and vitality by taking off his heavy garments and immersing himself in the waters. Water is a potent symbol in many scenes of everyday life in Japan today. For example, as soon as you take a seat in a sushi restaurant in Tokyo, the table will be wiped with a white cloth soaked in water. This has little to do with hygiene, rather it is an act of purification before rice is eaten.

Nothing evokes the feeling of clarity more for Japanese than seeing a fall of water against a mountain setting, preferably with a small shrine at the base of the waterfall.

THE MYTH OF AMATERASU HIDING THE SUN

Of the many stories recounted about Amaterasu, the tale of her withdrawal of labor is very well known. The most beautiful of Izanugi and Izanami's children, Amaterasu climbed the pillar connecting earth and heaven to rule the sky. Before he was banished to Yomi, her brother Susano announced that he wanted to say goodbye to his sister first. He was jealous of his sister's beauty and seniority and, wary of her brother's intentions, Amaterasu armed herself with a bow and arrow before meeting him.

Susano, however, charmed her by suggesting that they produce children together as a mark of good faith. Amaterasu agreed and asked for his sword. She snapped it into three pieces, and while crunching each bit in her mouth, created three goddesses with her breath.

SUSANU'S TRICKERY

Susanu asked for Amaterasu's five necklaces, which he chewed up to produce five gods. An instant custody battle ensued, as Amaterasu claimed them as her children since they were created from her jewelry. Her brother, however, thought he had tricked the sun goddess, and he celebrated by breaking down the walls of the rice fields, blocking irrigation channels, and then defecating in the temple where the

Right: The white sand and rocks precisely laid out in the garden of the 15th-century Ryonji temple are a fine example of Zen purity, a far cry from the bloodthirsty chaos surrounding the early Shinto legends.

harvest festival was to be held. His appalling behavior laid the seeds of their enmity.

THE DISAPPEARANCE OF THE SUN

One day, while Amaterasu was weaving clothes for the gods, Susano threw a flayed horse through the roof of the weaving hall, terrifying one of her attendants so much that she pricked her finger and died. Amaterasu herself was so scared that she hid in a cave, blocking the entrance with a huge bolder. Without the sun goddess, the world was plunged into darkness and chaos.

The paddy fields lay fallow, the gods misbehaved, and an assembly of 800 deities met to discuss how to lure Amaterasu out of the cave. They followed a plan introduced by Omobikane, the "thought-combining deity," who suggested that they should make her curious about life outside her dark cave. They decorated a tree with offerings and jewels, lit fires and drummed and danced, taunting her with the beauty of another goddess. They put a magical mirror outside the cave, collected roosters to crow outside it, and persuaded the goddess of the dawn, Amo No Uzume, to dance on it. Completely carried away, she started to take off her clothes, much to the amusement of the other gods, who called her the "terrible female of heaven"

As they had hoped, Amaterasu peered out to see what was going on. The gods replied that they were celebrating as they had found her successor, an even better goddess than she. Emerging from the cave, Amaterasu saw her reflection in the magic mirror and the "hand-strength male deity" Tajikawa pulled her out of the cave, blocking it to prevent her return. Nature was restored to life and since then the world has experienced the normal cycle of day and night. The mirror was entrusted to the mythical first emperor of Japan as proof of his divine power

The 800 gods punished Susano by fining him, cutting off his beard and moustache, tearing out his fingernails and toenails, and expelling him from heaven.

LAND OF THE RISING SUN

Japan was said to have been created by the will of the sun goddess Amaterasu, and the stark emblem of the Japanese flag shows the people's evident pride in these origins. The shrine of Amaterasu at Ise is still venerated, and every New Year thousands gather on the shore to watch the sun rise over the mountains. The tale of Amaterasu's return to the world is celebrated at a sacred cave, where a small round mirror symbolizes the alluring bronze reflection of the ancient legend. The mirror is a sun symbol throughout Asia.

THE IMPERIAL LINE

Amaterasu is supposed to be the direct ancestor of the Japanese imperial family and a mirror, the *Yata Kagami,* forms part of the imperial regalia. Pictures of her emergence from the cave show her holding a sword which she passed on to her grandson Prince Ninigi, which is another sacred part of the royal regalia. Amaterasu occupies a key position among the huge number of Shinto gods, and the obedience that was due to the emperor is echoed in the veneration of the sun goddess.

Right: A woodcut print by the 18th century artist, Hokusai of Tago-no-ura, in the series Thirty-six views of Mount Fuji. *Hokusai was one of the earliest Japanese artists to absorb European influences, daringly depicting everyday life as well as landscapes.*

Above: A play performed at the Sansen-in temple at Ohara, a mountainous region dotted with small villages. It depicts ancient gods and heroes.

Far right:A paper screen by the artist Ogata Korin (1658-1716), decorated with pink and white plum blossoms.

Amaterasu's shrine at Ise is the most important in Japan, and worshipers at the harvest festival, who pray to the "Great Heaven Shining Deity," incorporate blessings for the imperial family with their thanks for a fruitful harvest.

"As you have blessed the ruler's reign, making it long and enduring, so I bow down my neck as a cormorant in search of fish to worship you and give you praise through these abundant offerings on his behalf."

MOUNTAIN DEITIES

Japan is a mountainous country with over 60 active volcanoes, and is prone to earthquakes. In Tokyo it is not unusual to feel shocks every three days or so. It is not surprising, therefore, that the Japanese revere mountain gods, and almost every mountain has its own deity worshiped by the local people.

One of the most ancient mountain gods, O-Yama-Tsu-Mi, was born when Izanagi cut the fire god into four pieces at the time of Izanami's death. The most important is Sengen-Sama, the goddess of Mount Fuji, the highest mountain in Japan. Her shrine attracts many pilgrims who climb to the top of Mount Fuji at dawn to worship the rising sun and glimpse Sengen-Sama, who holds a magical jewel in her right hand and a branch of the sacred sakaki tree in her left.

CONCLUSION

The creation myths of Japan tell of a number of important deities and have their origins in the ancient folk religions of the region. Important though they are, the great gods of the sun, the moon, and the stars are not alone in the heavens. They are joined by an enormous number of lesser ancestral spirits, the *kami*, the Buddhas, and the bodhisattvas, who all seem to exist amicably together.

Left: The Gion Festival dates from the 10th century and is one of the biggest in Japan. It captures the collective spirit of the Japanese religion by offering prayers for the happiness of the people.

GODS AND GODDESSES

Previous page: Rengyoin temple was founded in 1164 and rebuilt in 1266 after a fire. It contains 1001 small figurines of Kwannon, known in China as Guanyin, the goddess of mercy.

Right and below: To the untutored eye it is very difficult to distinguish between Japanese and Chinese painting. The landscapes are very similar in form, and the Japanese were heavily influenced by the style of Chinese artists. These are part of a set of eight album leaves attributed to the 17th century artist Gong Xian (fl. 1656-82).

Shinto believers worship *kami*, or the divine forces of nature. *Kami* are anthropomorphic, with human forms and actions, and possess two souls: one gentle and one aggressive. Some live in heaven, some on earth, and because they are not omniscient, messengers are needed to communicate between the two. According to some calculations, there are more than eight million gods in the Japanese pantheon and their roles may sometimes appear to be rather confused as myths about them are quite regional and vary both from place to place, and between the various early written records

SHINTO HEAVEN

The Shinto heaven is simply a more beautiful version of Japan. It was initially linked to Japan by the heavenly floating bridge, but while the gods were asleep it collapsed, leaving only the isthmus west of Kyoto. This very straightforward, almost simplistic, view of the cosmos reflects the simple life of the early

Above: A fierce porcelain figurine of a four-legged, cloven-hooved thunder god. This may be part of a household shrine.

PRINCIPAL SHINTO GODS

Izanagi	First god of earth who created the world. Father of Amaterasu, Tsuki-yomi, and Susano
Izanami	Wife of Izanagi, and first goddess of the earth
Kagu-Zuchi	The fire god, also known as Ho-Masubi (or causer of fire). The last child of Izanagi and Izanami, his birth killed his mother. It was important to propitiate Ho-masubi during the Japanese windy season when wooden houses and buildings were prone to be destroyed by fire.
Amaterasu	Sun goddess and ruler of heaven
Tsuki-yomi	Amaterasu's brother and god of the moon
Susano	Wicked storm god and brother of Tsuko-Yomi and Amaterasu
Wakahiru-me	Younger sister of Amaterasu, probably a goddess of the rising sun
Kusa-nada-hime	The "Rice Paddy Princess" and wife of the evil Susano
O-Kuni-Nushi	God of medicine and sorcery; son of Susano
Ame-no-Oshido-Mimi	Son of Amaterasu, who she sent to control the earth, but he refused to go because it was too full of disturbances
Ninigi	Grandson of Amaterasu, finally sent to reign over earth
Kono-Hana-Sukuya-Hime	Daughter of a mountain god and wife of Ninigi
Takami-Musubi	One of Amaterasu's chief assistants
Amo-No-Uzume	Solar deity, thought to be goddess of the dawn
Inari	Rice god and god of prosperity

THE AFTERLIFE

The afterlife was a mysterious shadowy existence, with no hint of punishment for earthly sins. Buddhist beliefs changed this, and later Shinto legends acquired more hellish overtones.

THE GREAT SHINTO GODS

The most important gods in the Shinto pantheon are those descended from the creator deities Izanagi and Izanami.

Amaterasu, the sun goddess, is preeminent, and the myths surrounding her are the most important of the Shinto faith, the most famous being about how she hid the sun (see the previous chapter). Shinto is one of the few world religions to have a sun goddess, rather than a god. Amaterasu is a beautiful, benign goddess, who loves to send the life-giving rays of the sun to shine upon her worshipers.

Amaterasu's reign was challenged by her brother Susano, the storm god, the "valiant, swift, impetuous deity." After he had been exiled for his harassment of his sister, he wandered the earth. At Izumo he fought with an eight-headed serpent, which he managed to slaughter, cutting it into pieces. A sword fell from the monster's tail, and Susano sent it to Amaterasu as a token of his submission. This sword is now part of the royal regalia of the Japanese emperor.

Inari is the god of rice, and every Japanese village contains a shrine to him as the bringer of agricultural prosperity. When he entertained the moon god Tsuki-yomi, he ensured that the land was stocked with rice, the sea with fish,

Right: In order to ensure that a wish comes true, the Japanese purchase good-luck Daruma *dolls and paint in one of their eyes. If the wish is granted, they paint in the other eye as a sign of gratitude.*

Left: A Shigisan scroll from the Kamakura period (12-13th centuries) showing the ordinary lives of peasants. Agriculture, represented by the bullock, is never far away.

Right: Heian shrine in Kyoto. The Japanese acquired the pagoda structure of some of their shrines by adapting aspects of Chinese architecture. Built in 1895 to commemorate the 1100th anniversary of the Heian capital, the shrine is dedicated to the spirit of the Emperor Kammu (781-806). Every October, during the Jidai festival sacred to this shrine, worshipers dressed in historic costumes parade through the streets.

and the mountains with game. Tsuki-yomi was unhappy with the fact that these gifts had come from his mouth and rather ungratefully killed him. Life sprang forth from his corpse, however, as plants, cattle, and silkworms grew.

SHINTO SHRINES AND FESTIVALS

Kami inhabit the many Shinto temples and shrines that proliferate throughout Japan. Shrines are dedicated to different *kami,* so the rituals at each one vary slightly, but it is believed that the shrines act as forces for the revitalization of the *kami,* especially at New Year. Japanese people carry out acts of *matsuri,* a word which has come to mean "to serve the *kami,*" and which embodies the highly valued qualities of respect and obedience. Shinto encourages gratitude to the *kami* and to the ancestors, who are responsible for life and the blessings enjoyed by the living. The purpose of Shinto is to enact the will of the *kami,* the family ancestors, the community, and ultimately, the nation

During festivals the deity is carried out of

Right: A mythical kappa *emerging from a pool. Taken from a scroll painting in* The Compendium of Ghosts *by Bakemonojin, 1788.* Kappa *play a role in Japanese mythology similar to that taken by trolls and water spirits in western tales.*

the temple on a portable shrine, the *mikoshi,* and paraded through the streets. The procession allows the *kami* to protect and bless the community which worships it.

THE FESTIVAL OF RYUJIN

One of the most popular Japanese festivals is that of the dragon god Ryujin, god of the ocean. His festival takes places every June, and he is worshiped particularly by farmers, especially in time of drought. Many Pacific cultures revere a god of the ocean, and the mythology of Ryujin is typical.

Ryujin lives in a magnificent coral palace beneath the sea near the islands of Ryu Kyu. It is guarded by water dragons and he is served by the fishes of the sea. Controler of the thunder and rain, he is the most powerful of the *Raijin,* or weather gods. In his kingdom, a single day is equivalent to 100 human years, and on each side of the palace lie the halls of the seasons, both of nature, and of mortal life. The Palace of the Spring in the east has cherry trees full of butterflies, and the nightingale can be heard singing sweetly. In the south, the Palace of Summer is filled with lush vegetation and the sound of insects. In the Palace of Fall, the trees are beautiful shades of red and gold, and in the north, the Palace of Winter is a hall of eternal frost and snow, from which, however, there is no return.

MINOR DEITIES

The legendary figures known as *tengu* are among the most ancient mythological creatures in Japanese belief. It is believed that they inhabit trees in mountainous areas, particu-larly pines and cryptomerias. Part human and part bird, they are sometimes shown wearing cloaks of feathers or leaves, and often sport a small, black hat. *Tengu* love to play tricks, although this stems more from a sense of mischief than evil. Often, however, they fail to appreciate it when the joke is on them! A boy taunted a *tengu* by claiming he was able to see into heaven by using a hollow piece of bamboo as a telescope. The *tengu* was overcome with curiosity, and agreed to swap his cloak of invisibility for the stick of bamboo. When he found he had been deceived, the *tengu* took his revenge by causing the boy to fall into an icy river.

ONI

Oni are supposed to have come to Japan from China along with the Buddhist faith. They are fierce, horned devils, often of giant size. They are basically human in appearance, but have three fingers and toes, horns, and tails. Sometimes they also have three eyes. Whereas *tengu* are playful, *oni* are usually cruel, generally not very bright and often lecherous. They appear in many Japanese folk tales.

THE TALE OF MOMOTARO

Momotaro, revered for his nobility of spirit and accomplishments in battle, was born into a peach. A childless couple found the peach floating in a mountain stream, and on cutting it open, discovered a tiny baby boy. They named him Momotaro, which means "peach child," and brought him up as their own son.

When he was 15, Momotaro decided to repay his adopted parents and their neighbors

for their generosity. A number of *oni* lived on an island nearby and were making raids on the mainland to steal treasure and terrorize the population. Taking three rice cakes from his mother, Momotaro set off on his mission. On his way he met a dog, a pheasant, and a monkey who each agreed to accompany him in return for a rice cake. The band of four took a boat to the island of the *oni*, where they found a number of girls being held captive after being kidnapped and raped. With the help of his companions, Momotaro launched an attack on the *oni* stronghold, and killed all the supernatural beings. The boat was then piled high with stolen treasure and the prisoners released. Momotaro returned home in triumph, and was able to ensure that his parents lived out their lives in comfort.

Below: The faithful at prayer before an incense-burning altar at a Buddhist temple. Note the age of these people – Japan is becoming an increasingly secular society.

ISSUN BOSHI

Another diminutive hero is Issun Boshi, whose name means "Little One Inch." After many years of marriage, Issun Boshi's parents had not managed to conceive, so they prayed to the gods for a child, even one just as long as the end of a finger. The gods took them at their word, and Issun Boshi was born.

At the age of 15 (a significant birthday for tiny heroes, it seems) Issun Boshi set off for a trip to Kyoto, the capital. He took with him his parents' gifts of a rice bowl, a pair of chopsticks and a needle stuck in a sheath of bamboo. He traveled by river, using the bowl as a boat, and a chopstick as a punt.

On arriving in the city, Issun Boshi found himself employment in the service of a noble family. He worked hard for a number of years and entered the affections of his employers. One day Issun Boshi accompanied the daughter of the house to the temple. On their way two giant *oni* leapt out in ambush. Issun Boshi tried to draw attention to himself, thus enabling the girl to escape. When one of the *oni* swallowed him, Issun Boshi drew his needle from its scabbard and began to stab the *oni*'s stomach. He then clambered his way up the giant's gullet, stabbing with his weapon all the time. When he reached the mouth, the *oni* spat him out as fast as he could. The other *oni* lunged for Issun Boshi, but he jumped into its eye where he frantically continued to wield his miniature sword.

THE LUCKY MALLET

As the hapless devils retreated, one of them dropped a mallet. Recognizing this as a lucky instrument, Issun Boshi and the girl struck it on the ground and made a wish. Immediately, Issun Boshi grew to normal size and was magically clothed in the armor of a samurai, whose

martial attributes he had already shown himself to possess. On the couple's return, the father happily gave his permission for them to wed. Issun Boshi proved himself to be a devoted husband and brought his aged parents to Kyoto to share in his good fortune.

KAPPAS

According to some sources, the *kappa* is a creature descended from the monkey messenger of the river god. Resembling a monkey, but with fish scales or a tortoise shell instead of fur, the child-sized *kappas* are yellow or green in color. They inhabit rivers, ponds and lakes and have a hollow in the top of their heads in which sacred water is carried. If this water is spilled, the *kappa* is deprived of his magical powers.

Like vampires, *kappa* feed on human

Above: The classical Japanese Noh drama began in the Heian period (8th-12th centuries), was highly developed by the 14th century Ashikaga period, and is still very popular today. Noh ("masked theater") is a very stylized form of theater, with the main actors often wearing carved wooden masks. It developed from ceremonial religious dances, which were combined with monologs and dialogs.

blood, although they are also known to consume the blood of horses and cattle. As well as blood, *kappa* have a taste for cucumbers, and can be persuaded not to harm humans if a cucumber inscribed with the names and ages of the members of the family is thrown into the water in which they live. Their ability to keep a promise is a distinguishing and appealing feature of *kappa*s, as is their politeness. This is often their downfall, as when they bow down in respect, the water spills from the indentation in their heads, causing their strength to disappear.

THE *KAPPA* AND THE RIDER

A *kappa* who resembled a small child would ask passers-by to play pull-finger, and then drag its victims down into the pond in which it lived. A horseback rider agreed to play the game, but when their hands were locked, urged his horse into a gallop. As the water spilled from the *kappa*'s head it begged for mercy. In return for its freedom, the *kappa* promised to teach the rider how to mend broken bones. On being released, the *kappa* kept its word and taught the rider all it knew. The knowledge handed over by the *kappa* was treasured and passed down through generations of the rider's family.

BUDDHIST GODS

Buddhism coexists happily next to Shinto belief, and although about three-quarters of Japanese people are Buddhists, many also revere the Shinto spirits. The 15th century philosopher Yoshida Kanetomo stated that Shinto was the original trace and that the Buddhas are the fruit of its teaching.

All Buddhists venerate Gautama Buddha in their attempts to achieve Nirvana, but they also worship the various bodhisattvas who, in

Above: Yakushi-nyorai, "Lord of the Eastern Paradise," shown here flanked by two attendants in the Yakushiji temple in Nara. The statues were formerly gilt, but were blackened by fire in 1528. It was during the Heian period (794-1185) that Buddhist statues, which were normally made of wood, became formalized in Japan.

the manner of Christian saints, are patrons to particular causes.

Many people undertake pilgrimages to the various shrines of Buddhism, usually taking a route including 33 or 88 temples. In the past, pilgrimages were carried out in order to propitiate the gods, or to ask for special favors, such as good health or a successful harvest. They are yet another aspect of Japanese life which binds the people together with common values.

THE SEVEN GODS OF BUDDHISM

It was during the Kamakura period (12th and 13th centuries) that a truly Japanese form of Buddhism emerged. Honen and his disciple Shinran were responsible for the spreading of the *Jodo* school (or "pure land" sect) of Buddhism among ordinary people, and can thus take credit for its immense popularity ever since. Jodo made Buddhism accessible by arguing that one could achieve enlightenment by abandoning oneself to Amida Buddha, the "Buddha of Infinite Light." Popular Buddhism came to embrace many gods, or bodhisattvas, including the seven gods of fortune.

Hotei can be distinguished by his enormous pot belly, which overhangs his lower garments. Western assumptions of greed would be quite wrong, however, for Hotei's protruding stomach is a symbol of a soul that has achieved serenity through Buddhism, and an indication of its owner's contentment and good nature.

The god of longevity, Jurojin, is always depicted with a white beard and shown in the company of a crane, tortoise, or deer – which are themselves symbols of long life. He carries a staff from which hangs a scroll that contains the wisdom of the world.

Fukurokuju is easily identified by his odd

Above: A netsuke ornament showing the seven Buddhist gods of fortune in their ship. The popular gods of Buddhism made the religion more accessible.

He carries a sacred mallet with which he is able to grant wishes.

Another Buddhist god, who is sometimes regarded as a god of wealth, is Bishamon. He is always portrayed in full armor, carrying a spear in one hand and a miniature pagoda in the other – thus showing that he combines the virtues of a warrior and a missionary.

The qualities exemplified by the god Ebisu are those of honest toil. The patron of traders and fishermen, he is usually shown holding a fishing rod and his catch, a sea bream.

GODDESS OF THE SEA

The last of the seven is the goddess Benten. She occupies an important position among the group for she is associated with the sea. Many shrines to Benten are by the sea or on islands, and she is often portrayed riding a dragon or sea serpent. Benten is an excellent example of the ideals of feminine deportment and accomplishment in the arts, and she is often pictured playing a *biwa*, a mandolinlike instrument of which she is fond.

SOUL OF THE BUTTERFLY

This charming tale combines the Buddhist virtue of filial piety with the Shinto belief that all things, inanimate and animate, have a soul.

A young man and woman who shared a great passion for gardening were married. They lived together in great happiness, their love for their plants only surpassed by the pleasure they took in one another's company. Late in life they had a son, who fortunately inherited his parents' interest in plants. The couple died from old age a few days apart, while their son was still a youth.

The boy took over the responsibility for the garden, tending it with the care and devotion that he had learned from his parents. In the

appearance. He has a very long and narrow head, which is combined with a short and squat body and legs. He is also associated with the desirable attributes of long life and wisdom.

Daikoku is regarded as the protector of farmers. He is often shown seated on rice bales, which are sometimes being eaten away beneath him by rats. To this, Daikoku responds with his customary good humor, as he is so wealthy that he can afford not to be perturbed!

Above: When prayers are offered to Jizo, the guardian bodhisattva of children, these stone figures in a Tokyo Buddhist temple are dressed up to look like dolls. The bamboo canes support scrolls of prayers and invocations from worshipers. Jizo is believed to protect children and help the souls of dead fetuses, so the dolls are often purchased by women who have lost babies.

Right: Ink on paper painting by the monk Hakuin (1685-1768) of the Indian monk Bodhidharma, founder of the Zen Buddhist sect. His particular form of Buddhist spirituality has influenced all the Japanese arts, from calligraphy, to garden design, to the tea ceremony.

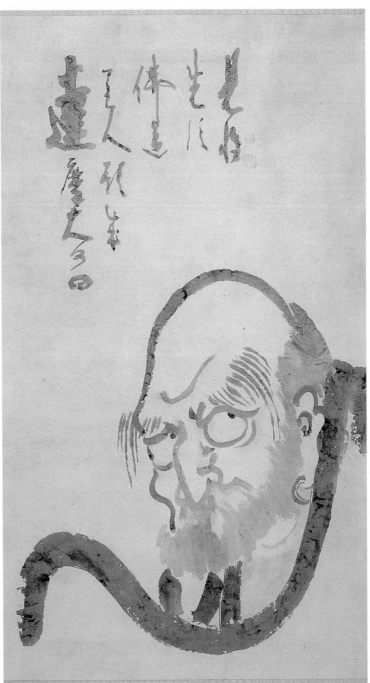

spring that followed their death, he observed each day two butterflies in the garden. One night he dreamed that his mother and father were wandering round their beloved garden, inspecting the plants they knew so well to see how they were faring in the boy's care. Suddenly, the old couple turned into a pair of butterflies, but continued their round of the garden, alighting on each flower in turn. The next day the pair of butterflies were still in the garden, and the boy knew that they contained the souls of his parents, who still derived pleasure from their life's work.

Left: A netsuke rat, one of the 12 animals of the zodiac, another of the many examples of Japan's cultural borrowings from China. Netsuke are exquisitely carved ornaments, originally used as fasteners or brooches.

Below: In front of the main building of the temple, and marking off the area of the gods, hangs the shrine nawa, *similar to a large rope plait, made from rope that has been ritually purified.*

GREAT LEGENDS

The Japanese civilization is not as ancient as that of its nearest neighbor, China, and the influence of Chinese legends on Japanese mythology is immense. The great legends of Japan incorporate aspects of Confucianism, Buddhism, and the earlier animist beliefs in the power of nature and divination. As the power and authority of the emperor grew stronger in the 8th century, the supporting myths became more universal and were gathered into two great collections, the *Kojiki* and the *Nihon-shoki*. These books became the basis for later Shinto authority and contained the fundamentals of the national religion.

FUJIYAMA

During the medieval period, Japan was riven by civil strife, and the peaceful coexistence between Shinto and Buddhism was dented slightly by the rise in the 16th and 17th centuries of patriotic nationalist sects. They taught that Japan was the center of the world and that Mount Fuji, the sacred spirit mountain, was the guardian of the nation. These teachings, however, were rooted in Shinto legend

THE APPEARANCE OF MOUNT FUJI

An old man who grew bamboo trees on the slopes found a baby girl called Kaguya-hime, and he adopted her and brought her up. Exceptionally beautiful, she became the consort of the emperor, but seven years after the marriage Kaguya-hime told him that she was not, after all, a mortal, and that she must return home to the heavens. To alleviate her husband's sadness she gave him a magic mirror in which he could always see her face, and then she disappeared.

Devastated by his wife's absence, the sad emperor decided to follow her to heaven, and, clutching the mirror, climbed the slopes of Mount Fuji. On the summit there was no sign of the princess. The emperor was overwhelmed by his love for her, which burst out of his breast and set the volcano alight. From that day, it is said, smoke has always risen from the top of the volcano.

THE BIRTH OF PRINCE NINIGI

The grandson of Amaterasu, Ninigi's parents were Ame-No-Oshido-Mimi and his wife Taka-Mi-Musubi. Ame-No-Oshido-Mimi had declined to intervene in the troubles of the earth, and Amaterasu, worried by the plagues that beset the people, sent Prince Ninigi to rule over them.

Amaterasu gave him jewels and the sword of his uncle, the storm god Susano, to help him in his endeavors. His sister, Amo-No-Uzume, goddess of dancers whose realm is the floating bridge linking heaven and earth, accompanied him through the clouds, and he was also guarded by legions of warrior

Previous page: Cherry blossom is one of the emblems of Japan, and features in many legends as a symbol of spring.

Right: Mount Fuji is the sacred mountain of Japan. According to legend it was created by an earthquake in 286 B.C.

Above: The warm climate of the island of Hinoshina near Hiroshima is perfect for agriculture. Many of the great Japanese legends are about efforts to control the forces of nature through the gods.

deities. Ninigi arrived on earth on top of Mount Takachihiat at the point where eight earthly roads lead away in every direction, and was confronted by the mighty god who controls all pathways. Amo-No-Uzume intervened on her brother's behalf, and Ninigi was shown all the kingdoms of the earth. In gratitude, Ninigi allowed his sister to marry this god.

Prince Ninigi chose Ko-No-Hana, the goddess of flowers and of the sacred Mount Fuji, as his wife. Guardian of the elixir of eternal life, her father is Oho-Yama, the mountain god, who tried in vain to persuade Ninigi to marry Iha-Naga, his elder daughter instead. Ninigi and Ko-No-Hana lived together happily for several years and produced three sons, but

Ninigi's jealousy eventually ruined their relationship, and his wife committed suicide.

Their sons, however, went on to found the Japanese royal line, from whom the present-day emperor is descended.

FRATRICIDE WITHOUT REMORSE

This tale is taken from the second book of the *Kojiki,* the 8th-century collection of the legends of Shinto.

Among the many children of Emperor Keiko were the brothers Opo-usu and Wo-usu, the second of whom was later named Yamato-takeru. One day the emperor sent Opo-usu to summon two maidens who were renowned for their beauty. But instead of summoning them, Opo-usu made them his wives and sent others in their place. When the emperor learned of his son's betrayal, he ordered Wo-usu to persuade his elder brother to come to dine with his father. Five days passed, but there was still no sign of Opo-usu. When the emperor asked Wo-usu why his brother had not come to court, Wo-usu explained simply, "I captured him, grasped him, and crushed him, then pulled off his limbs, and wrapping them in a straw mat, I threw them away."

FORCE AND MORALITY

This example of brute strength without any regard to morality explains why Yamato-takeru is seen as an embodiment of natural force, that

Below: A bout of Sumo wrestling may only last for a few seconds. The contest ends when any part of the combatants' anatomy apart from their feet touches the floor. The reverence felt for Sumo wrestlers can be linked to the admiration felt for the mythical figure of Yamato-takeru, master of gods and men.

is beyond the understanding of a mortal being. Nature brings about harvest, and at the same time can be utterly destructive. It is to be admired and feared.

Throughout, the style of the *Kojiki* is realistic, and often cruelly bloody. This violence is in evidence throughout the adventures of Yamato-takeru, as he is sent by his father the emperor to quell both real political enemies, and also "unruly" deities. Japan's indigenous sport, Sumo, is also characterized by its display of sheer power.

SUMO WRESTLING

Wrestlers are often very quiet people, and are expected to live simply. We can see in Sumo the same sort of admiration as that shown for the boy-hero Yamato-takeru. There are many elements of Shinto ritual in Sumo. Wrestlers throw salt before each bout to purify the ring. They use water put beside the ring to clean their mouths, symbolizing the purification of their bodies. The ring is made of packed soil in which various symbolic items are placed dedicated to the gods.

YAMATO-TAKERU'S TRAVELS

Yamato-takeru next embarked on a long journey, as the emperor dispatched him to destroy rebel forces.

First he was sent to the west to kill two mighty brothers; when he arrived at their house he found it surrounded by rows of warriors. Yamato-takeru was so young (perhaps only 15 or 16) that he was able to disguise himself as a young girl by combing down his hair and

Left: A splashed-ink landscape by the 15th century artist Sesshu. The accompanying text explains how he went to China to learn this particular technique.

dressing in women's clothes. He went into the house while the feast was taking place. The brothers were very pleased to see this "girl" and had her sit between them. Then, when the feast was at its height, Yamato-takeru seized one of the brothers by the collar and stabbed him clear through the chest. The younger brother quickly ran, off, but Yamato-takeru seized him and stabbed him too.

CLEANSING BY FIRE

On his return home, Yamato-takeru subdued and pacified all the mountain, river, and sea deities, but it was not long before the emperor commanded Yamato-takeru to deal with more unrest in the east. Yamato-takeru went to his aunt, Yamato-pime, complaining that he was being sent out again too soon, and without adequate protection. On his departure,

Below: The traditional dance theater Kabuko, which is enacted by men only, has been popular since the 17th century.

Above: Prints by Utamoro (1754-1806) of young women visiting the seashore at Ise, the site of the shrine of the sun goddess. At New Year the sun rises between the twin rocks, joined by a straw rope which marks the boundary of the territory of the gods.

Right: A sliding-door painting from Chisyaku-in temple in Kyoto, showing the traditional contemplative qualities so popular in Japanese art and central to both Buddhist and Shinto beliefs.

Yamato-pime gave him a sword and a bag, and said "Should there be an emergency, open this bag."

After conquering his father's enemies, Yamato-takeru met a man in the land of Sagamu who deceived him, saying that an unruly deity resided in the middle of the plain. When Yamato-takeru entered the plain, the man set fire to the area, but Yamato-takeru escaped using his aunt's bag and sword. He mowed the grass with his sword, then lit another fire with a flint which he found in his aunt's bag. Then he killed the man and all his clan, burning the bodies.

One of the imperial treasures of Japan is a sword. A sword is one of the symbols of the figurehead of Shintoism, because it symbolises lightning: thunder is regarded as promoting good harvests, since the amount of thunder, and consequently rain, has most to do with the growth of rice. The idea of the gift of fire is so widespread that it would seem to be practically a part of the "collective unconscious"

Above: The puppets used in Bunraku theater are manipulated by three people, clearly visible behind a narrow stage.

or racial memory. It appears in the legends of many cultures – consider the Greek Prometheus myth, for example.

THE DOWNFALL OF YAMATO-TAKERU

As Yamato-takeru crossed the sea, the deity of the crossing stirred up the waves, creating a storm, and the boat began to drift helplessly. His wife, Oto-tatiban-pime, offered to sacrifice herself to the sea god in his place, and stepped out on to the flimsy layers of sedge-mats, skins, and silk carpets spread out on the boiling waves. As she went down on to them, she sang:

O you, my lord, alas –
You who once, standing among the flames
Of the burning fire, spoke my name
On the mountain-surrounded
Plain of Sagamu!

Seven days later, Oto-tatiban-pime's comb was washed ashore. Her body was never recovered. Taking this comb, her grieving husband made her a tomb and placed it within it.

YAMATO'S DEATH

Yamato-takeru then experienced the first of the incidents that lead to his downfall. On his way back to the capital, when he was eating his rations at the foot of the pass of Asi-gara, the deity of the pass, assuming the form of a white deer, came and stood next to him. Yamato-takeru struck the deer with the leftovers from his meal, hitting the deer's eye and killing him. Then he climbed up the pass and, grieving, sighed sadly three times:

Below: A Buddhist cave painting at Dunhuang depicting a group of mourners at a funeral. These paintings are strongly influenced by Central Asian and Indian artistic traditions.

"My wife, alas!"

He was defeated by the deity of Mount Ibuki, who caused a violent hailstorm which dazed Yamato-takeru. His mind recovered a little as he rested at a spring, but because of his extreme fatigue he walked along slowly, using a staff. He proceeded across the plain of Tagi to the plain of Nobo, where he sang this song recalling his homeland:

From the direction
Of my beloved home
The clouds are rising
Next to the maiden's
Sleeping place
I left
The saber, the sword –
Alas, that sword!

He died. When his family came down to the plain of Nobo to construct his tomb, they also sang:

The vines of the Tokoro
Climb around
Among the rice stems,
The rice stems in the rice paddies
Bordering the tomb.

The *Kojiki* has many beautiful songs such as these which anticipate the Japanese poetical forms *waka*, or *haiku*. They are symbolic rather than descriptive, their simplicity attempting to capture emotion or instantaneous thought without using words of emotion. The above song is meant to capture the desolate

Left: The delicate architecture of this building in Kyoto, the ancient capital of Japan, exemplifies the contemplative nature of many Japanese arts.

feeling of people everywhere who have lost the man they loved.

Excluded from the Divine
Transformed into a giant white bird,
Yamato-takeru flew away toward the beach
followed by his family:

Moving with difficulty, up to our waists
In the field of low bamboo stalks,
We cannot go through the skies
but, alas, must go by foot.

As they waded into the sea, they sang:

Going by sea, waist-deep in the water

We move forward with difficulty
Like plants growing
By a large river
We drift aimlessly
In the ocean currents.

Again when the bird had flown to the rocky shores, they sang:

The plover of the beach
Does not go by the beaches
But follows along the rocky shores

These concluding songs to the story of Yamato-takeru express the destiny of earth-bound humans. The exclusion of man from

Above: Like so many aspects of Japanese culture, tea was introduced from China. Zen Buddhists believed that tea was an aid to meditation, and during the Ashikaga period tea-drinking developed into a highly stylized ritual, often taking place in a building specially constructed for the purpose.

61

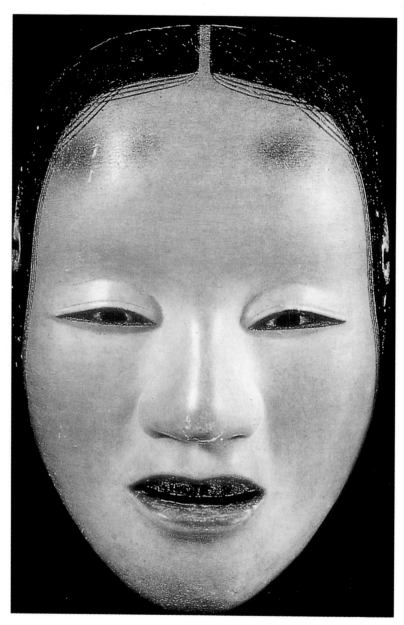

the realm of the divine, and his struggle to re-turn, is common to many mythologies from around the world. Some authorities believe that in this tale the flight of the bird is con-nected to the tradition of mourners dressing as birds to sing and dance at funerals. It is ei-ther an attempt to call back the soul that has flown away, or else intended to assist the soul of the deceased in its ascent to the higher celestial regions.

THE FISHER BOY

Japanese myths feature many marriages between humans and divine, or semidivine, beings.

A young mortal named Urashima married a beautiful sea maiden and lived with her hap-pily in a watery palace beneath the waves. After several years, he was desperate to see his par-ents again, so his wife gave him a casket, which, if left unopened, would enable him to return to the deep.

When he arrived back in his native land, Urashima was dismayed to find that several centuries had elapsed since his departure, and he opened the lid of the casket. A puff of white smoke blew out of it and drifted away toward the sea, while he was shaken by a bitterly cold wind that turned him into an ancient man and then a corpse. Today the shrine of Urashima stands on the coast of Tango.

THE UNDERWORLD AND AFTERLIFE

Early Shinto belief had no concept of souls undergoing judgement after death for the deeds committed during their life on earth. Emma

Left: The wooden mask of a Noh *play, worn by an actor playing a middle-aged woman in the 15th century drama* Fukei, *by Tokuwaka.*

O, the lord of the dead, is largely a Buddhist creation, and derives from the Hindu Vedic god of death, Yama. The Japanese still celebrate *Bommsatsuri,* the Festival of the Dead, every July, when lanterns are lit to guide the dead on their journey to another life. Restless souls who wander the earth are known as *Shito Dama,* and can sometimes be seen by the human eye as glowing spheres.

THE DEMON ROAD

After death, the soul must travel for judgement to the Yellow Springs, the realm of Emma O in the underworld kingdom of Yomi. It is a long journey and the dead are given food and money. When they arrive at Sanzu-No-Kawa, the dried up river of the dead, they must pay Sodzu Baba, the old woman who controls the crossing.

When the soul arrives in purgatory, or Gakido, "the Demon Road," it is judged according to the Law of Buddha, and must atone for sins committed on earth. This is the lowest point in the soul's existence. Only the intervention of the benign goddess Guan Yin can exonerate a soul and ensure its passage to a peaceful eternity, and this is only likely if a person has passed a blameless existence on earth, preferably visiting all 33 shrines to Guan Yin which are scattered round Japan. Guan Yin can also lessen the penance due to a mildly wicked person. The truly evil, however, face the wrath of Emma O, who throws them into a vat of molten metal.

The god Jizo also protects souls by guarding graveyards and keeping the *oni,* or evil

Left: A guardian figure at Horyuji temple at Nara, the oldest-preserved temple complex in Japan and a fine example of the architecture of the Asuka period (552-645 A.D.).

spirits, at bay. Jizo hides souls in his robes to prevent *oni* from snatching them, and helps souls in purgatory by shielding them from the punishments of Emma O.

A MULTIROOTED MYTHOLOGY

Prince Shotuku (572-621), who engineered the first official Japanese contacts with China in 607, later compared the three philosophical systems of Japan to the root, the stem, and branches, and the fruit and flowers of a tree.

Shinto, the native religion, provided the roots, which are embedded in the earth of the folk tradition. Confucianism provided the healthy branches of social order and learning; and Buddhism was the blossoming of religious spirituality. The three belief systems intermingled and have produced a rich mythological heritage that still plays an important part in Japanese life.

Shinto, which is inextricably linked to the power of the ruling family, has remained the focus for national aspirations, while Confucian ethics provided moral rigor. The arrival of Buddhist literature stimulated the evolution of Japanese legends and folklore, enriching the ancient tales and providing new stories.

Left: The elaborate rooftop of the Heian shrine, founded in 1895 to celebrate Kyoto's 1100 years as Japan's capital.